KT-528-302

Scenes Of Moderate Violence

SCENES OF MODERATE VIOLENCE

JOHN MOYNES

This edition first published in 2019

Unbound
6th Floor Mutual House, 70 Conduit Street, London W1S 2GF

www.unbound.com

Text Design by PDQ

A CIP record for this book is available from the British Library

ISBN 9781789650372 (trade paperback)
ISBN 9781789650389 (ebook)

Printed in Great Britain by Clays Ltd, Elcograf S.p.A

1 3 5 7 9 8 6 4 2

MIX
Paper from responsible sources
FSC® C018179

In memory of Danny and Eoin Rogers who now reside with the Gods.
They were adored and loved and are missed more than mere words
could ever convey.

Super Patrons

Christopher Baum
Karen Bhreathnach Uí Chuinn
Conor Bofin
David Braziel
Willy Brennan
Carol Burke
Mairia Cahill
Michael Cahill
Úna-Minh Caomhánach
Dermot Carroll
Charlie Connelly
Mick Corrigan
Aoife Cox
Gemma Craddock
Maura Culbert
Michael Cunningham
Eoin Cunningham
Angeline Deaton
Richard Delevan
Broadsheet dot ie
Darragh Doyle
Daniel Dunne
Terry Dunne
Greig El Irish
Brian Emmet
Jack Fox
Helen Francis
Will Gaughran
Gale Gilbert
Verity Halliday
Fiona Hanley
Robbie Haycock
Mick Hodgkin
Maria K
Noreen Kehoe
James Kelleher
Fiona Kenny
Dan Kieran
Rory Leahy
Zohar Lee
Barry Lyons
Anne-Marie Manton
Peter Mc Hugh
Karen McCormack
Brian McDonagh
Julian McElhatton
Jacqueline McEwan
Simon McGarr
S J McGarrigle
Kevin McGee
Nick McGivney
Colin McGovern
Bernard McGuiness
James McNulty
Lucy Michael
Frank Miler
John Mitchinson
Emmet Moorhouse
Vera Moynes
Stephen Moynes
Adrian Moynes

James & Vera Moynes
Remy's Musicfilmblog
Niamh Ni Chonchubhair
Avril Ni Dhúill
Brian Nisbet
John Nisbet
Liz Nugent
Cian Ó Muilleoir
Feargal O'Connell
Colm O'Gorman
Ciaran O'Rourke
Leo O'Shaughnessy
Desmond O'Toole
Damien Owens
Justin Pollard
Eoghan Rice
Alex Robertson
Danny Rogers
Mary Frances Ryan
Johannes Scharlau
Tommy Smith
Deborah Staunton
Brendan Strong
Emer Tilson
Nicola Timmins
Saoirse & Niamh Tobin
Colm Tobin
Shaun Usher
Katia Valadeau
Ian Walsh
Shona Weymes
Susan Wilde
Fiona Wilde
Adrian Wilson
Allan Yates

Scenes Of Moderate Violence

Instructions

Just think of this book as a western
And know you'll find no wisdom here
For this is a page, not a lecturn
If you're travelling east then I fear
That the stories I tell will not bring you
Any peace or enlightenment or
If just once you think my words ring true
I'm telling a joke. Nothing more
Than a man who can just about handle
A metre, a line and a rhyme
Not a prophet who walks with a candle
And guides you past space, beyond time.
These rhymes at their best, they are what they are,
Mere trifles to learn and recite in a bar.

On The Economic Implications Of The Continental Breakfast

In civilised locations like Belfast or Rathkeale
A gentleman can wake up and eat a decent meal
He'll start with half a dozen eggs and then begin to dig
Into a dizzying array of things made out of pig.
His cousin on the continent, Pedro, Pierre or Fritz
Begins his day not in this way but staring at some bits
Of sliced up fruit, a little cheese, a small cold square of meat
A thimble of espresso is his meal's only treat.
So Paddy's cursed to start his work already satisfied
His mind at rest, his belly full, his urge to strive has died
While European industry, fuelled by a tiny meal
Is why they make cars by the Rhine, but never in Rathkeale.

Two For The Price Of One

You remember old Chicago, before the West was won,
When you brought your steers to market, you also brought your gun,
For they always tried to cheat you, but once your work was done,
You'd peel a few bucks off your roll and go and have some fun.

For long rough months you'd dreamt of this, the north end of the trail,
For long tough months you'd thought of nought, but one cold sip of ale,
Each time you held your hat against a roaring icy gale,
Your mind slipped off and focussed on one pleasure that can't fail.

Some say that in Chicago bars, men don't sit and converse,
In fact their favourite pastime almost borders on perverse,
I'll admit they keep their clothes on but that somehow makes it worse,
They just gather round a poet, and hear him read bad verse.

You walked into a dive like this, the honky tonk stopped dead,
And as the patrons stared at you a shifty scoundrel said,
"Well Stranger you look like a man who thinks himself well read,
So you'd better have a poem or two for us within your head."

"The work of Yeats I like" he said "and it would be a crime,
To forget old Philip Larkin, so angry yet sublime,
I said I want a poem or two, so you'll give us a rhyme,
From both of these great poets, both at the same time."

The mob began to bet and sneer, and laugh and jeer and gloat,
You knew you had to get this right, you didn't dare misquote,
Though you couldn't think of one damned line that either poet wrote,
But the mood was getting ugly so you stood and cleared your throat.

They will arise and go now, your mum and dad,
They may not mean to go to Innisfree,
They'll build a hut with bricks they had,
And add a shelter for a bee.
And they shall have some peace there, from fools in old style coats,
Who half the time were soppy, at where the cricket sings,
There midnight, at each other's throats,
Sternly full of linnet's wings.
I will arise and go now, give misery to man,
I hear salt water lapping, down by the coastal shelf,
So go stand by a roadway, or pavement while you can,
And go to Innisfree yourself.

In that bar in old Chicago, where this sad tale began,
The mob were not impressed. At least you faced them like a man,
You shot two before they brained you with a heavy frying pan,
But you knew as you lay dying, you'd made your last poem scan.

For Hamish

Well Hamish now you're mostly lying on your
Back and burping, smiling, reaching for an outstretched finger
Grasp it now. Your Father, Mother
Gave you gifts I know will linger
On. When life is hard and things go wrong
And things go wrong, they do that without fail
You'll take it, and you'll make things right. You're strong.
And in the future when we share an ale
And you complain about the fights you fought
I'll groan along and we will both pretend
You made yourself, and you were never taught.
Just know this clan will stand here and defend
You. All we want is that someday we see
You go have fun, run wild, stay safe, be free.

The Choir

At the centre of the ship was a choir that sang forever
The choristers wore slippers of the softest kind
So when their shift was over they could leave their place
And be replaced by a fresh voice without disturbing the song
The conductors too were changed at intervals the next one
Standing beside and following the beat for a minute or two before
The change of a movement when they'd step in and the other
Would leave to sleep or to teach new conductors.
The song had endured unabated for seven hundred years
At first there was a weekly song, a way for workers to forget
The idiocy of this task. Twelve years in and they're just past Jupiter
And the choir becomes a daily event at the centre of the ship
Later, still near enough the start of the long gap they got the news
That what was left of Earth wasn't there any more and accelerating
Through generations of nothing but the vast ship and the vast hope
Of everyone on slender shoulders and the song stopped stopping
There were captains then but now the ship is steered by singers
We passed six planets with cool air, seas wet and ground hard
A seventh comes and before it goes the song will come to an end
And good people and soft slippers will be hoist by my petard.

Childish Things

In the sunshine long ago
I asked my grandmother
What London was like in the war
She said that when the sirens went
They'd go down into the tunnels
I stamped my feet, said No.
I'd read all that. I wanted facts
About what war felt like in the heart.
She smiled and stuttered and couldn't speak
My questions seemed so clear to me
But mud to her as soldiers went
About their business at the end of the road.

Tally Stick

We made sticks to hang
Around the necks of kids
To beat them when they used
The language of their parents.
We made examinations
To break the hearts of kids
And fail them when they used
The language of their parents.
We made shite of both our tongues
And so we blame our kids
And curse them when they sing
The language of themselves.

Tuesday

Last Tuesday out of want
Of anything else to do I meddled
In the affairs of wizards.

Of course I can remember
In primary school being told not to meddle
In the affairs of wizards.

And I've seen the ads on television
Warning us not to dream of meddling
In the affairs of wizards.

Last Tuesday I discovered
It's a tedious waste of time to meddle
In the affairs of wizards.

Tuam

We kill the children of unwanted mothers,
Now hold your tongue and do not speak so fast,
Those women were a stain upon their brothers,
And anyway you cannot judge the past,
Back then, you see, and here you must agree,
Death didn't hold the fear it does today,
Shame did, and so no one could ever see,
A victim with a chance to get away,
Unbranded and then maybe build a life,
Unpunched by nuns. We know that way,
Was barred to sluts. She should have been a wife,
Before the rape. She knew the rules. Her choice,
Was made. There's nothing to be gained,
By half arsed token efforts to give voice,
To those who had to die while old rules reigned.
So close your eyes, recite the savage lie,
Those prone to sin must watch their children die.

Mind The Past

In this decade of centenary,
We speak of days of yore,
Domesticate obscenity,
Rehearse the ways of war,
With all the sensitivity,
Of gunmen at your door.

Imposters

I once gave myself to Failure
To her kiss, her skin, her hair,
And I always will love Failure
I'm just having an affair.

You know that sometimes fools like me
Let lust disolve our continence
But never fear a fool like me
Just trust in my incompetence.

For sometimes in my line of work
The best laid plans blow up
I did my normal kind of work
And saw Success show up.

So just for now I love her
This sexy, sacred cow
But I will not always love her
Or forget my sacred vow.

That I gave myself to Failure
To her kiss, her skin, her hair,
That I always will love Failure
I'm just having an affair.

Green Shoots

I know this is the wrong time of the year,
Though that's a very foolish thing to say,
The winter falls, but I've found cause for cheer,
I may have turned a corner yesterday,
And when and if I did I saw green shoots,
A hint of confidence come back again,
And fear, of course, for vulnerable grass roots,
I know how quickly they can wither when,
I trick myself and think the healing's done,
This small good news won't leave me overjoyed,
No tiger roars, this race is not yet run,
While half my feelings still are unemployed.
The shoots are green, which means the news is good,
And I reacted as I know I should.

The Ballad of Tim Berners-Lee

At the arse end of the eighties, a young Tim Berners-Lee,
Invented a new language which he called HTTP,
And from this clever code of his the modern world was born,
It changed how we communicate, and gave us lots of porn.

And though he was a genius, this great Tim Berners-Lee,
Perhaps he would have stayed his hand, if only he could see,
That a foul and loathsome creature, malevolent and cold,
Would creep onto the internet and lurk beneath the fold.

The first words on the world wide web came from Tim Berners-Lee,
He fired them down a phone line to some remote PC,
That machine, though unattended, replied to Tim to say,
That he was bald and stupid, and fake and fail and gay.

I beg all engineers to think, of poor Tim Berners-Lee,
And when inventing anything, include a guarantee,
That their shiny new creation won't let the world forget,
That society has nothing if it has no etiquette.

September 2013

Let's worship the men of the Lockout,
And praise all that Jim Larkin said,
The tram workers now are all heroes,
They're heroes because they are dead.

Spare a thought for those men on that brave day,
When they stood before Murphy's dread rage,
Then shut up and bring me my latté,
Or I'll lower your minimum wage.

It baffles me now that mere workers,
Once could purchase a house or a car,
It's time to clamp down on those shirkers,
We have to, we are where we are.

We'll have no more talk of progressing,
To this one truth we'll always hold fast,
That union men are a blessing,
As long as they stay in the past.

Anonymous

First we admit that we are powerless over literature, that our lives have
 become meaningless.
Then we came to believe that only a power greater than ourselves could
 restore us to clarity.
And so we decided to turn ourselves over to the care of an editor, as we
 understand them.
We made a searching and fearless inventory of our vocabulary.
We admitted to our editor, to our ourselves and to another poet the exact
 nature of our typos.
We prepared our poems for submission.
We humbly asked our editor to remove our clichés.
We made lists of all persons we had harmed.
We wrote verses of apology to our victims.
We continued to draft, redraft and start to write again.
We sought through reading and reciting to improve our conscious contact
 with Heaney, Joyce and Yeats as we understand them.
Having had a literary awakening as the result of these steps, we went to
 Grogan's, and told everybody.

That's Me Told

I'm told there was a time when certain foreign forces ground us down,
They did. That's true.
I'm told there was a time when we were all to blame for what went on,
That we all knew.
I'm told that now these crimes will be debated and decided on,
Then made anew.

Safely At Night

Buy stocks in hats, cloth sacks, and caps,
Knitted with thick wool, long enough to pull,
Down below the chin, holes to let the light in,
For soon rough men will buy them.

Winston was lying, those rough men,
Don't visit violence on our foes. They stand,
Prepared do the worst because they can, and,
If you can't stop the killing, turn a shilling.

The First Night Of The Festival

I'm standing in Ireland's most expensive nightclub
The price of a cocktail here would get you
Half hammered in my local
And my local isn't cheap.
I'm shouting in Ireland's most expensive nightclub
Holding a microphone surrounded
By the sleek clean youthful joy
They say the Germans stole.
I'm reading in Ireland's most expensive nightclub
Roaring about the wrong socialism
To people who don't and won't need
The safety it offers.
I'm failing in Ireland's most expensive nightclub
Where instead of preaching the glamour
And danger of Che Guevara
I give them Jack O'Connor.
Behind me in Ireland's most expensive nightclub
A jazz trio improvise and know
That it's a long way from saxophones
I was reared.

Boys At Play

Back in a purer, nobler age
The least of us was ranked a sage
He cared enough about the stage
To risk arrest and Yeats's rage.
That riot had a quiet charm
And in the end it caused no harm
The most who shrieked with fierce alarm
Next praised the least when he took arm.
The least spilled blood so he could clean
The stage and set a better scene,
Give later lessers draped in green
The right to sue a handy queen.
These shabby modern writ dispensers,
Pale shadows of heroic censors.

Come Of Age

I grind my teeth in silent rage
As laughter swirls around the bar
And all my anger comes of age

I stare but do not read the page
My foes are happy where they are
I grind my teeth in silent rage

I built this bitter dead-end cage
I bought each frigid iron bar
Before my anger came of age

As arseholes make themselves a stage
Each thinking he's a superstar
I grind my teeth in silent rage

And though I've never earned a wage
I'm better than these shits by far
And so my anger comes of age

I yearn to be an angry phage
Reduce their insides to a scar
I grind my teeth in silent rage
Enjoy my anger come of age.

The Waste Years

A century since Kipling wrote
Epitaphs: Common Form.
A century since we mattered.
A hundred years of dancing
After Eliot, into the Wasteland.
A hundred years of wanking.
We had an audience once
We have professors now.
But we had an audience once.
You've studied the classics?
Well done. I've not. I won't write poems
For people who've studied the classics.
We had a crowd once
Now people are paid to understand us.
We have whores now.
Don't question why our market died
It was murder, and worse, suicide.
And no one fought and no one tried.

Infestation

We found scratches on the skirting board
Bite marks on the back door and small piles
Of gold appeared in our cupboards
In the garden ribbons arrived
Tied around the stems of shrubs
And the rosemary we never use
We called a man who poked around
Sucked air through his teeth and said
Yeah, you have a leprechaun
There's a part of me that thinks
Nature should be left alone
But there were bites and scratches
And all that gold. The bloody gold
It has tax implications it causes
Problems a householder can't endure
Poison was deployed by the man
And traps as well in case the beast
Had evolved some sort of immunity
A week later I found the leprechaun
Its neck snapped by the neighbour's cat
But we still had to pay the man.

Dedicated To A Friend

I do enjoy your company
As much as I hate your verse
But to offer an empty compliment
Is to burden myself with a curse
And so I'll play the jester
And keep the humour running
The only defence I allow myself
Is violent freestyle punning.

True Story

In Brussels in June she told me
That she might not be there the next day
Like a fool I shouldered my musket
And nodded and marched away
Years later we first met in Dresden
We kissed on the very first day
And collapsed in a muddle of elbows
As the fire bombs burned us away
Before we were eaten by hatred
When love was the light of each day
We snogged and we groped and we fumbled
On a bridge over Thermopylae
There's a scar on my face from a laser
My leg's lost to a plasma array
You met an artillery major
You flew home with that bastard that day
Now I pick up my axe and my crossbow
And I put on my helm and I say
That the enemy's here so we will go
And make them regret this day
Now fetch me a bottle of vodka
And fill my canteen to the brim
I can't forget about her
And I must not think of him.

Noble Failure

I've gazed at blank pages perhaps more than you
Blank screens are more common, but they're still the same
When I picked up a square foot of canvas
I signed up to a trickier game
I learned to smear paint on toy soldiers
They have angles and corners and rules
You've a mission before you start marching
You're not standing up proud with the fools
Who set out with only a figment
And somehow turn that into art
Who splatter some dearly bought pigment
To show you the shape of their heart

Consequences

A lonely hare upon a hill
A drunkard in a chipper
A fleeting unimportant thrill
A pirate's favourite slipper
A boy who thinks his boyfriend
Is playing silly games
Someone who phones a journalist
And won't name any names
Right now an eager five year old
Has made a dreadful plan
Embrace your fears. It ends in tears
Kids will do what they can
An owl upon a treetop
A coward on a wage
Hold prey in sight all through the night
With misdirected rage
Now run directly from this place
And tell your favourite daughter
What happens to these things
Matters more than Irish water

Escape

We got her out of Galway
Before the priests arrived
Rumours had reached Romish ears
That ancient craft survived
In an electrician's van
We hid the frightened crone
And drove her through the priestly ranks
To the liberated zone
We'd sworn that we'd keep witchcraft safe
From Temple, Church and Kirk
The struggle was the point
We know witchcraft doesn't work
Inside the liberated zone
We begged the witch to stay
She climbed upon her broomstick
And flew home to Galway.

Uniform Blackness

Over pints of uniform blackness
I told some learned sots
That I once composed a villanelle
About how much I hate the Trots.
This line set no tongues wagging
In the fashionable parts of town
But you know you've said something brilliant or daft
When Tom Mathews writes it down

Bad Advice

Six straight white guys
Sitting in a bar
Each setting the whole world to right
Each sipping on a jar
They're all good men but if you'd let
Your life run free and far
Sit down and plan and don't forget
Straight white guys in a bar.

Drunken Bakers

Two of Disraeli's angels
Hewed from perfect vibrant stone
Who boiled a billion bagels
Kneaded fingers to the bone
And also sometimes needed
A day or so's relief
From a God they prayed and pleaded
For an honest chance, one brief
Enough to earn a clear way out
Make their lives fine and dandy
God gave them discount watered stout
And Tesco's Own Brand Brandy
Move on, don't waste another glance
At port stained chins and shitted pants.

People Die Of Exposure

They say that every poet knows
Nineteen names for every plant
Dictates where every river flows
Swaps gossip with each lowly ant
They say we dine on meals of air
Get drunk on mere exposure
Earn cash without a single care
By bleating at a crozier
They say it's easy, simple and
We pocket money every day
I will admit my life is grand
But I'll insist not one of They
Has read a poem since they got warm
By burning their school uniform

Pillar

He told me, "Edith, we must flee
And when we flee we can't look back
Our God saw things he would not see
Those sinners all deserve the flack.
They got obsessed with filthy cocks
And wallowed in forbidden beds
Ignore the million burning rocks
Jehovah sent upon their heads."
There were no millions, only three
Small falling stars, so round a stone
I crept and scurried back to see
What I could love when left alone.
Lot lost himself among the sand
I found myself. I'm feeling grand

Prepare To Fail

The old mistake. We thought this war
Would be just like the last
So we marched out with weapons
That conquered in the past.

Last year we fought each other
And both saw victory
But we were both defeated by
Nights in, watching TV.

The Northern Office

I'm the youngest, the rest are retired
Some took it early, but most of them are late now
A few of them are at the age, but artists
They wouldn't retire if they could afford to.

A pub is a place to medicate failure
And those I meet with all know success
A good pub is a temple of loneliness
Where wise men pray in company.

Warning

A sign hung in The Project Arts Centre.
"This video installation contains
Scenes of mild nudity."
Did the author of that sign
Ever sit supping pints
With his friends of an afternoon?
"I met this girl on Friday night
In Whelan's. We went back to hers
And lads, she was pretty mild."
I want to meet him in the final reel
And explain my feelings
In scenes of moderate violence.

From Folly Bridge

Take a boat, from Folly Bridge to Godstow
And just float, while tiny hands that can't row

Make you steer, and under pressure be
Politely queer, so now while speaking free

You will give birth, to Jabberwocks and Queens
A better earth, two dozen happy scenes

Cards marked and Kings castled
A cat's smile as logic's rassled.

Funny Friday

We are the people who stay up
Far too late, shivering in bedsits
Studying Hardy, Laurel and Cooper
Arguing over the perfect way
To deliver a custard pie.
We are the people who obsess
Ourselves with the crucial question
Of which edit of Ad Nauseum
Actually got the balance right.
We are the people who get annoyed
In Grogan's when someone misquotes
Chris Morris or, worse, Groucho.
We are the people who kissed goodbye
To house and car and kids and pension
So you could tap an arm in a pub
And pass on someone else's joke.
We are the people who sacrificed
Nothing. We knew the scorpion before
We picked it up and the sting we suffer
Is a lifestyle choice.

Armies Of Me

I met myself the other day
In someone else's words online
A me that wandered far away
From this me, this mere starting line.
What armies have my actions made?
What flattened doppelgangers thrive?
What twisted, partial, me-loud glade?
What rotten self defeating hive?
Have my words birthed in other minds
Just regiments of rank decay?
Or are there mes of other kinds
With something positive to say?
I own these mes, their hopes, their fears
Less than the me between my ears.

Negotiation

In the ninth hour of the ritual
When your arms are tired
And the incense stings your eyes
And your throat is raw from chanting
And reality shatters and borders break
And a demon stands before you
If you've done everything correctly
Sanctified the space, hallowed the chamber
Removed all the impurities, the many impurities
From your will and your desire
When you've filled the cup with your own blood
And given it to the demon to drink
Then and only then can you bargain
Over nine longer hours parsing
Every word, every offer, ensuring
That you aren't walking into a trap
You built yourself for eighteen hours
That now at last you have the power
To make your people's wishes real.
Some fucker outside the temple will say
He could have got a better deal.

Roosevelt's Heirs

There aren't really many types of weapon
Sword, spear, rifle, rock are all
Merely ways of focussing force
On a single point.

Bombs are the other way
Bombs and flamethrowers
Their force affects an area
And not a single point.

Bombs are unpredictable
And flamethrowers downright awkward
The winner is he who deploys
The maximum force in the precise place

Roosevelt, in the Oval Office
At some point said Yes
Holding a proposal
To change the rules.

D Day happened at high tide
Nobody can or would ever again
Muster like that, put that much force together
We'll not see its like again.

Roosevelt's heirs are focussed
Thrusting spears and firing rifles
At precise points behind the blindfolds
They choose to wear.

A Road

Is that flat white or americano?
Drive, cycle or bus? I don't care
Once or twice a decade you go
Somewhere, but yellow trees are rare.
And a forest? An entire yellow wood?
It never happens. It's not untravelled
You'd be lucky if somehow you could
Find the path before the wood unravelled
And all the rest, all broken, spinning
Accept this horrid dreadful gyre
Don't ever let your meagre sinning
Excuse a living funeral pyre
Brutal, savage, short is all
I don't fit in, I'm far too tall.

Most Weeks

Have I spent enough of my life yet
Staring at unanswered emails
Waiting for unwanted phone calls
Opening uncalled for envelopes?

There will be a war next week

Surely a point must come
When a bell rings and a firm clear voice
Announces that I've done enough
And can take the rest of the day off

There will be a war next week

I know the options. I've read brochures
It's a vale of tears or all life is suffering
Or nature red in tooth and claw
The dreary struggle for genetic survival

There will be a war next week

Stop it. I'm not asking for new rules
But surely it is not beyond the pale
To expect a bordered sanctuary
I could visit for a little while

There will be a war next week

Would you ever fuck off?
I'm aware there will be a war next week
There was one last week, and the week before
Weeks have wars. I'm doing a poem now.

There will be a war next week

I know. I am familiar with military history
And I happen to quite enjoy it
The names, numbers, uniforms, stories
Are fine in their place. In history.

The war next week is your fault

No. No, it's not my fault and can't be
I did my bit with banners, protests, pamphlets
Not just against the bombs and the tanks
But against the systematic economic inequalities of—

The war next week is your fault, you tired old lefty cliché

You can stick that up your arse
And fuck off while you're doing it.
A secondary voice playing the role of my conscience
Has no right to call me or anyone else a cliché.

I'm not your conscience I am the voice
Of a tireless, fearless, endless horde
Revenants of your mistakes, your trespasses
Bringing you a message you must hear.

Oh. Will there be a war next week?

There will be—ah, yes, as you say, a war next week
Not in some foreign sandy place or jungle
Where Americans slaughter at will, but closer
To your home and heart and all behind your eyes

Go fuck yourself.

Your childhood, Michael Buerk in Ethiopia
Flies crawling on an infant's eyes
Grainy footage of shooting in Romania
Grey horrors that stalked your own streets

This ends here. I've done my years
Raising awareness of mental health
Telling jokes about capitalism to the comfortable.
If money was disease I'd be immortal

There will be a war next week

I don't care. Not any more. I'm tired
Of poems that don't rhyme and want
To make the world a better, fairer place
And haven't the decency to include a joke.

There will be a war next week

Bite me.

Dead Ends

There was a girl once, and she was beautiful
And I wasn't close enough to fall in love
Pleasant as that would have been. Her hand
Landed on mine and politely moved my arm away.

A gentle advance countered by a firm rebuff
Is not that bad. It's not a poem.

There was a girl once who invited me in
More than close enough to fall in love
And the end, the confused polite hatred
Of two incompatible coincident traps

Had a poem or two or six in it.
I wouldn't read them or pick up a pen.

A Dream Of Leaving

Leave me a space, a small space
Without chink or width or wonder
A small room for small thoughts
That will be aired or thunder
Smash the village burn the art
The rest. Evil must be excluded
From the world and exclusion
Means management and so
Ultimately thought must be
Left a little corner for itself
A reserved space for reserved sins.

It Must Be A Lovely Feeling

Administration on this job
Is, for now, delayed.
We need what you are doing
But you will not be paid.

You understand this industry.
You've been around the block
You've slept with so much banditry
This won't come as a shock.

You'll die as poor as you are now
Or die in much more debt.
Your corpse assured that no demand
Has been or will be met.

The point of all this freedom
Has not and won't be made.
We'll take what you are making
And you will not be paid.

Nostalgia

There was a girl once, long ago
A teenage girl, and pretty
And I was teenage and there too
In love with the last girl I saw and so

Nothing happened. Things happened, as they did
And didn't in those days. But nothing happened
Not with her. I never tried to embarrass myself.

Years later, in a café in another country
She said that back then she liked me
But thought I was out of her league.

When she told me that it didn't matter
We were both older, both happy, both seeing
People we would be with forever.

Back then I didn't think anyone could imagine
A league below the one I played in,
Briefly on the occasional Sunday
When someone else was injured.

I never told her, in that café
In the other country, that back then
I thought she was out of my league.

Because she had handed me something awful
The worst turd you can hold in your hands
The sure and certain knowledge that you could have been happy once
But you fucked up and it's all your fault.

I could have told her, and she'd have taken no offence
That I fancied her back then. But the turd
It's not something you'd hand to someone
Who never did you any harm.

On Barton Road

On Barton Road one night
I'm walking home, after a couple of pints
And I see a young woman
Walking towards me on her way wherever.

There's a wide enough pavement
On Barton Road, and the grass goes out even further
There's a lot of space there
So I gave it to her. All the space in the world.

And as I pass her on the outside
I glance and see fingers fisting in fear
There was a wall on her other side
And all I offered was a flanking manoeuvre.

I walked on. I didn't look back
There was no other escape to give her
And without autohagiography
I've never wished any harm on a stranger

I'm used to constant fear
Of strangers. I'm big and tall and shambling
And I can just about suppose
That I seem a threat to those who think like me.

I saw those fingers curl to fists
And generally I don't. But they'll curl and curl
For Barton Road is a world
With gardens that we cultivate.

For Now

Roads curve and paths loop and shortcuts
Take you the wrong long way and every so often
I'm back in the dead place, the romper room.
Let's keep this as a metaphor. Let's ignore the fact
That the first thing I see in the morning
Is a wooden chest of drawers with a sharp corner
I once cracked my forehead off after doing something daft.
Ignore the blades and knives I keep on the desk
Beside my bed. They're there for silly reasons my hobbies
Require ploughshares I once bent to other ends.
This old terminal cavern is a place I know too well
I've been called here more than once
And I'll answer that call again. But sometimes
A twist of thought can summon me
When I'm not in a mood where the darkness can bite
And I stand in the grey light of a pregnant crypt
Behind the tombs of failed crusaders they gather
A parody of claws and teeth and mucus
And tentacles that snap back, burned by the grey light.
This is a silly place so I leave, turning my back on all this
Bullshit, for now.

The Old Jokes Are The Worst

Spine straight and shoulders back
That's the way to stand
When you're curled foetal on the ground
A scalpel in your hand

And face the razor's narrow width
Between defeat and the right choice.
That blade is the wrong metaphor
And mine is the wrong voice.

Water, Water, Everywhere

You will not win, you can't, I'm holding every card
You'll work so much and get so close you'll see the sight
Of rocks above the waves. You'll work that hard
And do that well. I'm straight and male and white.

And middle class. And I speak in the perfect way
You know that now. And I live in a slum
I built through years of effort. You will say
You kicked so hard, and couldn't pass the scum.

Ante Diluvium

Careful triangulation
Will reveal the place to stand
One hill in this low nation
Is the highest moral land
Between the pure frustration
Of extremist pundits and
The national castration
That the ruling classes planned.

You And Your

You
You and your made up issues
I'd achieve things
If I wasn't busy
Correcting you.

The Wreck Of The Erebus

Two feet planted two foot apart
Your arms braced against the bulkhead
The magnetic locks in your boots engaged
The hull ruptures and you've already seen
Comrades with less protection hurled into the void
Where the vacuum boils their saliva
As their eyes freeze and shatter.

Two feet planted two foot apart
You can't reach out without disturbing
Your balance. And balance matters
I keep reaching and almost grab
Whispers of tired science fiction
So empty my saliva boils
And what's left of my vision shatters.

We've All Had Days At Work Like This

I mean, I could, if I wanted to
Give you a few nice lines
In the same way I once learned
To write a joke and sell it
When I wasn't in the mood
I could muster up some references
To regiments that did something
Or mention a painting in a place
That about half of you have been
Even without dipping into depression
Which still has a year or so in fashion
Or left or feminist, and that reminds me
I could riff on woman. The poem woman
You know. The bullshit.
But poetry must and will be taken seriously
So I'll—actually, this will do.

Thank You All

Lend me a fiver and we'll burn down the church tonight
No, I won't have dinner with you and your girlfriend today
I'm back with the ghosts and the aliens and occasionally
I'll emerge gloriously to dance for money I won't ask you for.

When I climb out, and sometimes I climb out, and then
You'll act as if these interludes are all I am and the months
Of gross offence are just like that time that guy left his shoes behind
Panic pauses terror takes the night off and I get to taste your air.

The End

I have nothing left
No plan, no horse, no moustache
Everything went
On one roll in a casino I knew
Was crooked.
If I could do it all again I'd—
No. No, I wouldn't
Someone else can make the trains run on time
Someone else can teach you shit
Give me one more go around
One chance to fix each of my million mistakes
And I'll take it with a smile
And walk back in
To a casino I know is crooked and leave
With no plan, no horse, no moustache.

Unbound is the world's first crowdfunding publisher, established in 2011.

We believe that wonderful things can happen when you clear a path for people who share a passion. That's why we've built a platform that brings together readers and authors to crowdfund books they believe in – and give fresh ideas that don't fit the traditional mould the chance they deserve.

This book is in your hands because readers made it possible. Everyone who pledged their support is listed at the front of the book and below. Join them by visiting unbound.com and supporting a book today.

Derek Ball
Mark Beynon
Aoife Carroll
Alan Duff
Conor Farrell
Tara Flynn
Jacky Grainger
Ray Harman
Niamh Hayes
Donna Hennessy
Naomi Hooban
Jane Lawlor
Phil Lynch
Christian Mainz
Maurice McElroy
Paul Moloney
Stephen Neil (PaddyAnglican)
Cormac Ó Foghlú
Carol Sherry
George Topping
Julian Willis
Sasha Wilson